On the Road

Ratios and Proportions

Nola Quinlan

Consultants

Pamela Dase, M.A.Ed.
National Board Certified Teacher

Barbara Talley, M.S.
Texas A&M University

Publishing Credits

Dona Herweck Rice, *Editor-in-Chief*
Robin Erickson, *Production Director*
Lee Aucoin, *Creative Director*
Timothy J. Bradley, *Illustration Manager*
Sara Johnson, M.S.Ed., *Senior Editor*
Aubrie Nielsen, M.S.Ed., *Associate Education Editor*
Jennifer Kim, M.A.Ed., *Associate Education Editor*
Neri Garcia, *Senior Designer*
Stephanie Reid, *Photo Editor*
Rachelle Cracchiolo, M.S.Ed., *Publisher*

Image Credits

Cover Getty Images/Blend Images RM, (inset) Max Krasnov/Shutterstock; p.1 Getty Images/Blend Images RM, (inset) Max Krasnov/Shutterstock; p.3 ollirg/Shutterstock; p.4 Blend Images/Getty Images; p.4–5 wandee007/Shutterstock; p.5 (top) Adam Jones/Getty Images, (bottom) LaiQuocAnh/Shutterstock; p.6 lana rinck/Shutterstock; p.6–7 rarena/Shutterstock; p.7 (left) LisaInGlasses/iStockphoto, (right) Sportlibrary/Shutterstock; p.8 (top) corepics/Shutterstock, (bottom) Henryk Sadura/Shutterstock; p.8–9 Sergey Mironov/Shutterstock; p.9 (top) Daniel Padavona/Shutterstock, (bottom) NatUlrich/Shutterstock, (inset) HomeStudio/Shutterstock; p,10 Mikhail Nekrasov/Shutterstock; p.10–11 Baevskiy Dmitry/Shutterstock; p.12 Massimiliano Pieraccini/Shutterstock; p.12–13 Denis Roger/Shutterstock; p.13 (top) Theodore Littleton/Shutterstock, (bottom) Ritu Manoj Jethani/Shutterstock; p.14–15 Worldpics/Shutterstock; p.15 Ministr-84/Shutterstock; p.16 katatonia82/Shutterstock; p.16–17 BedoMedo/Shutterstock; p.17 John Czenke/Shutterstock; p.18 (left) Spiderstock/iStockphoto, (inset) sosha/Shutterstock, (bottom) Yellow Dog Productions/Getty Images; p.18–19 gabczi/Shutterstock; p.19 DSGpro/iStockphoto; p.20 (inset) md0yl32/iStockphoto, (right) Karin Hildebrand Lau/Shutterstock, (bottom) Flickr RF/Getty Images; p.20–21 Frontpage/Shutterstock; p.21 BlueOrange Studio/Shutterstock; p.22 (left) wildarrow/Shutterstock, (right) Jose Alberto Tejo/Shutterstock; p.22–23 africa924/Shutterstock; p.23 Sailorr/Shutterstock; p.24 (top) Dvanphoto/Big Stock Photo, (bottom) Ye/Shutterstock; p.25 JustASC/Shutterstock; p.26 (top) loong/Shutterstock, (bottom) Philip Lange/Shutterstock; p.26–27 Nolte Lourens/Shutterstock; p.27 (top) Getty Images/Blend Images RM, (left) Getty Images/Blend Images RM, (right) Gary Yim/Shutterstock; p.28 WendellandCarolyn/iStockphoto

---

Teacher Created Materials

5301 Oceanus Drive
Huntington Beach, CA 92649-1030
http://www.tcmpub.com

ISBN 978-1-4333-3450-4
© 2012 Teacher Created Materials, Inc.
Reprinted 2013

The classroom teacher may reproduce copies of materials in this book for classroom use only. The reproduction of any part for an entire school or school system is strictly prohibited. No part of this publication may be transmitted, stored, or recorded in any form without written permission from the publisher.

Table of Contents

The Open Road	4
Getting Ready to Go	6
Roadside Stops	14
Road Trip Necessities	20
Off We Go!	26
Problem-Solving Activity	28
Glossary	30
Index	31
Answer Key	32

The Open Road

Do you take a car to get to school, soccer practice, or the grocery store? For many people, driving is necessary to get from one place to another each day. Traveling in a car can be frustrating when there is traffic or for people who have a long **commute** to work or school. Many people don't think of driving as fun.

Yet when it comes to planning a vacation or a special trip, traveling in a car can be part of the fun. Taking a road trip can make your next vacation even more exciting and adventurous!

Traveling by car allows you to explore in ways that you could not from a plane or train. You can see places and landscapes that may be new and interesting to you. Road travel can be unpredictable and carefree. You never know where you may end up!

Popular Road Trips

There are many famous **routes** that people like to travel by car. Historic Route 66 stretches more than 2,000 miles (3,219 km) across the United States from Chicago to Los Angeles. The Pacific Coast Highway in California winds along the central coast. The Flower Route in the Netherlands makes a beautiful springtime driving trip. The Pirate Route in Jamaica takes travelers on a historical journey through the island.

the Flower Route in the Netherlands

Did You Know?

There are over 600 million cars on the road worldwide. That's one car for every 11 people!

Getting Ready to Go

One reason that a road trip is unpredictable is because the things you encounter on the road are always changing. You can travel from bumper-to-bumper traffic for hours in the city to a quiet, **desolate** (DES-uh-lit) road in the wilderness. You might drive on a straight road that goes right through the middle of a desert and then reach a windy road that takes you through a mountain range. Other travelers you see on the road are always different, as well. Not everyone is in a car to take an exciting trip to a new location. Many drivers and passengers are just going about their daily lives. Drivers may be commuting to and from work. Truck drivers are likely hauling their cargo from one point to another. Construction workers are out to maintain roads, and law enforcement officers are around to keep people safe.

What Is a Ratio?

A **ratio** (REY-shee-oh) compares two quantities. For example, if a parking lot had 3 trucks and 6 cars, the ratio of trucks to cars could be expressed as 3 to 6, 3:6, or $\frac{3}{6}$. The ratio of cars to trucks could be expressed as 6 to 3, 6:3, or $\frac{6}{3}$.

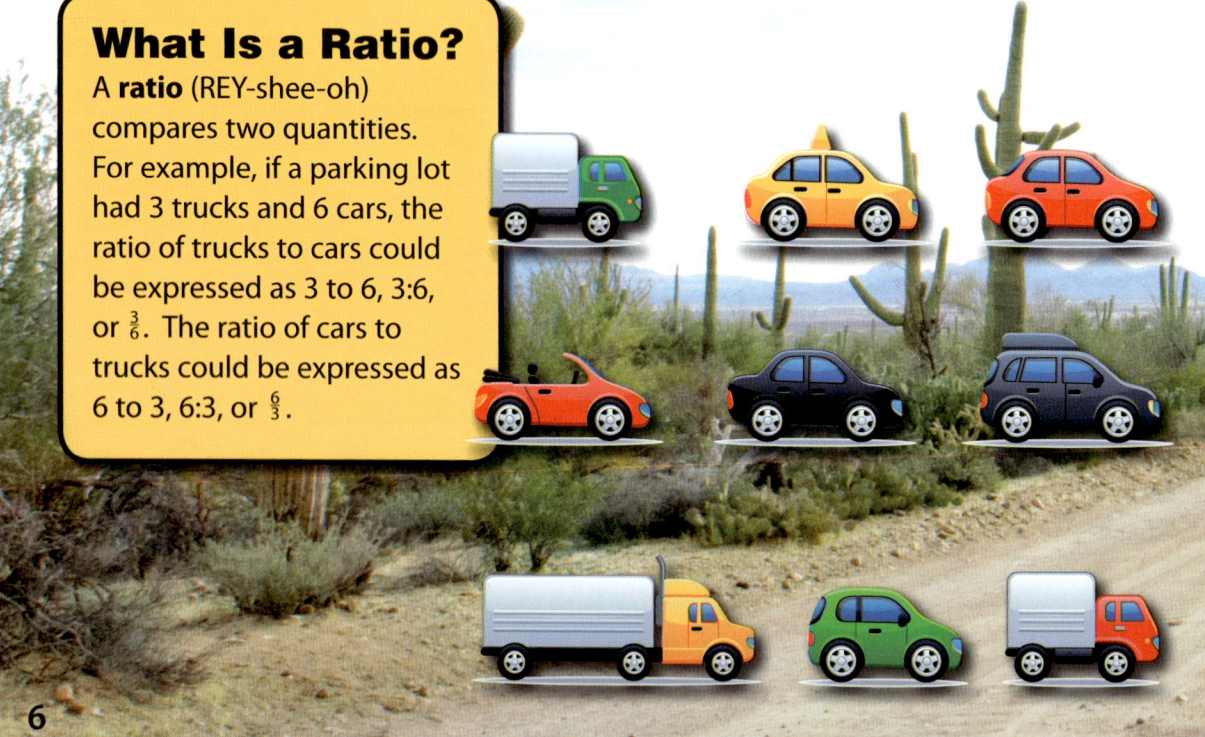

Equivalent Ratios and Proportions

Ratios can be simplified just like fractions. The ratio 12:15 can be simplified to the ratio 4:5 by dividing each part by 3. The ratios 12:15 and 4:5 are called **equivalent ratios**. A **proportion** is an equation formed by two equivalent ratios.

LET'S EXPLORE MATH

On a long road trip, Mr. Elliot wanted to keep his children, William, Malika, and Terell, occupied. He told William to count white vehicles, Malika to count red vehicles, and Terell to count black vehicles.

Later in the day, William reported 60 white vehicles, Malika reported 80 red vehicles, and Terell reported 90 black vehicles.

a. Express the following ratios in simplest form:
- red to black vehicles
- black to white vehicles
- red to white vehicles

b. Is the ratio of red to black the same as the ratio of black to red? How are they related?

c. How many vehicles did they count all together?

d. Express the following ratios in simplest form:
- red vehicles to the total vehicles counted
- total vehicles counted to black vehicles

e. Why is it necessary to express a ratio in words?

A successful road trip begins before you even start the car. It begins by researching and choosing a great place to visit. You plot your route by considering your starting point and your destination. Then you can decide what places to visit along the way. If you want to see more sights, you can choose a different route going and returning. Planning a road trip is a fun part of the adventure.

Cartographers

People who make maps are called cartographers (kahr-TOG-ruh-ferz). Designing maps requires a great deal of technique and precision. Though most maps today are created using computers, they still need to be updated as physical and political changes occur around the world.

A cartographer surveys the land to make an elevation map.

8

Finding Your Way

Most travelers on the road use maps to help them find their way. But maps have changed a lot over the years. Some people still use folding paper maps. Many travelers use road atlases, online maps, and **global positioning system (GPS)** devices.

GPS

The route you choose can be mapped down to the smallest detail. But it can also be just a rough outline of where you want to go. The beauty of a road trip is that there is flexibility along the way to change your plans. If you discover that you particularly enjoy one of your stops, you can always stay there a little longer. If one of your stops is disappointing, you can get back on the road a little quicker.

The stops along the way are the highlights of any road trip. Much of the time is spent gazing at the changing landscapes outside the window. Yet between those moments, you can visit small towns, large cities, and everything in between. Road trips allow you to get to know the world around you.

Some stops may require days. Others may be enjoyed in a few hours. Some travelers may choose their road trip stops based on people they know. They might have a friend or relative in one of the cities on the route, so they may plan some time for a special visit with that person. Other travelers choose stops based on their interests. They research a geographical area to find out what is interesting to see and do there. Hikers may look for the best walking trails, while art lovers may seek out museums.

Egyptian Museum in Cairo, Egypt

The two "end" numbers in a proportion are called *extremes*. The "middle" numbers are called the *means*.

means
3:5 = 12:20
extremes

Writing Proportions

When you write a proportion, it is important that the two ratios describe the items in the same order. Suppose you know that there are red and black cars at a rest stop and the ratio of red cars to black cars is 5:8. If you know that there are 50 red cars at the rest stop, you can find the number of black cars by writing the proportion $\frac{5}{8} = \frac{50}{y}$. Notice that the number that represents red cars is on the top of each ratio and the number for black cars is on the bottom. In order to get from 5 to 50, you multiply by 10. To keep the ratios proportional, you also multiply 8 by 10.

$$\frac{5}{8} \cdot \frac{10}{10} = \frac{50}{80}$$

There are 80 black cars.

LET'S EXPLORE MATH

On one day of the Elliot family's trip, Malika observed 75 blue cars and Terell counted 50 green cars.

a. Give the following ratios of the cars in simplest form: blue to green, green to blue, blue to total cars, and green to total cars.

b. Suppose that they continued to count, and the ratio of blue to green cars remained the same. Terell counted 150 green cars. Write a proportion that could be used to find the number of blue cars. How many blue cars would Malika have counted?

c. Suppose they counted a total of 240 cars. If the ratio of green cars to total cars stays the same, write a proportion that could be used to find the number of green cars. How many green cars would Terell have counted?

d. Using the information from problem **c**, how many blue cars would Malika have counted? How did you find the number of blue cars? How else could you have found the number of blue cars?

Once you know your destination, route, and a few interesting stops you would like to make, you will have a complete itinerary. Your itinerary is your plan for how you will travel and the order of places you will visit.

An itinerary can always change, but it is smart to have a general sense of the sequence of your trip. This plan helps you make sure there is something for everyone to enjoy on the road trip. The stops you make should be as diverse and unique as possible. You may also balance days that will be mostly in the car with days that include several stops. There is no faster way to get tired of a driving adventure than by having the same schedule day after day!

Cross-Multiplication

Another way to find a missing quantity in a proportion is to use cross-multiplication. In every proportion, the product of the extremes is equal to the product of the means. Let's say you are asked to solve the following proportion for *x*:

$$\frac{3}{6} = \frac{x}{8}$$

Using cross-multiplication, set the product of the means equal to the product of the extremes:

$$x \cdot 6 = 3 \cdot 8$$
$$6x = 24$$
$$\frac{6x}{6} = \frac{24}{6}$$
$$x = 4$$

If you draw a line from 3 to 8 and *x* to 6 you can see why this method is called cross-multiplication.

$$\frac{3}{6} \bowtie \frac{x}{8}$$

Road Trip Through Montreal, Canada

Departure: Montreal, Canada

Day 1: Mont-Royal and Downtown
- Visit Saint Joseph's Oratory
- Visit art museum: Musée des Beaux-Arts de Montréal
- Lunch in the Latin Quarter
- Tour the Underground City

Day 2: Vieux-Montréal and Maisonneuve
- Visit Notre Dame Basilica

Saint Joseph's Oratory

Speeding Car

The speed that a car travels is an example of a **rate**. The speed of a car is usually described in miles per hour (mph) or kilometers per hour (km/h). That means the average number of miles (kilometers) traveled in one hour. However, speed could be described in other ways: feet per minute, miles per minute, inches per second, or meters per day. Basically, you can describe speed with any measure of distance per any measure of time.

Notre Dame Basilica

Montreal Biosphere

LET'S EXPLORE MATH

On a trip, Mrs. Garcia traveled 168 miles in 5 hours.

a. Write the ratio (in fraction form) that describes Mrs. Garcia's rate. Simplify the ratio to find the number of miles she traveled per hour.

If she continues to drive at the same rate (constant speed):

b. How far could she travel in 12 hours? Write a proportion to solve the problem.

c. How long would it take her to travel 190 miles? Write a proportion to solve the problem. Round your answer to the nearest hour.

Roadside Stops

Ever since cars have been common and families started taking road trips, roadside attractions have appeared alongside our highways and freeways. Some of these stops are necessary to help the drivers on the road. Gas stations, for example, are always found along our busiest roads so that drivers do not have to go far to fill up their tanks.

Travel stops provide a hot meal and a place to rest for truck drivers who log long hours behind the wheel. Some travel stops even have hot showers for them!

> A **percent** is a special kind of ratio. It is the ratio of a number to 100. For example, 20% means 20:100 or $\frac{20}{100}$. To solve any percent problem, rewrite it in the form: ____ is ____% of ____. Write a proportion to answer the question *What is 20% of $30?*
> $$\frac{x}{30} = \frac{20}{100}$$

Most travelers on the road stop for meals. Restaurants are frequently found right off the road, often with signs and billboards that help point drivers in their direction. The fast-food industry has become a big business because of road travelers. Drive-through windows allow tourists to get meals quickly.

Travelers spend money at roadside stops, and they often spend more than the cost listed in a menu or posted on a sign. Tipping and sales tax can add a lot to road-trip **expenses**. Tipping restaurant servers is not required, but many people choose to leave 15 to 20 percent of the cost of the meal. Sales tax varies from region to region, ranging from no sales tax to a tax of more than 10 percent of the price of items purchased.

LET'S EXPLORE MATH

At a roadside stop, Keiko bought a T-shirt at a **discount** of 20%. If the regular price of the shirt was $18, how much was the discount? Solve the proportion $\frac{n}{18} = \frac{20}{100}$.

The discount is $3.60, so the shirt cost $14.40. Remember that if you take 20% off, 80% remains. You could also have found 80% of $18.

a. If Keiko's sister paid $15.00 for her T-shirt and received the same 20% discount as Keiko, what was the original price?

b. Keiko's brother got a better discount on his shirt. It originally cost $20, and he paid $12.00. What percent discount did he receive?

Look closely at the stops that are available alongside highways. You will notice that they are not just essential businesses that help drivers get from one place to another. Roadside stops can also be tourist attractions. They are generally interesting places that are destinations themselves.

one of the largest flower clocks in the world, Kyiv, Ukraine

Cadillac Ranch in Amarillo, Texas

Some attractions are in odd locations that prevent people from just driving by. In order to lure travelers to stop there, some roadside attractions are quite unique or quirky. People may stop to see something that they cannot see anywhere else. For example, if you stop in Plano, Texas, you might want to visit the Cockroach Hall of Fame. If you are ever in Duncan, British Columbia, you can see the world's largest hockey stick and puck. There are also replicas of Stonehenge all over the world that attract tourists. Stonehenge replicas have been made from cars, foam, and even old refrigerators!

the world's largest spider in Ottawa, Canada

Helping the Economy
A small tourist attraction can be instrumental in helping a local **economy**. If you own a roadside stop, then you depend on visits from tourists to help keep the doors open. Once people come to visit your business, they may also spend money on gas, food, or a hotel. That helps other business owners in the area.

Despite all of the interesting places to stop on a road trip, there is still going to be a lot of time spent in the car. There is really no way to avoid that on a road trip. Some people enjoy being in a car for a long period of time. Others do not. Luckily, there are many ways to help pass the time while you are cruising down the highway.

> Dominique spent one hour listening to music for every two hours she spent journaling about her trip. The ratio 1:2 represents this relationship. To determine how many hours she spent listening to music after 8 hours of journaling, write the proportion $\frac{1}{2} = \frac{x}{8}$. Solve the proportion to find that she listened to music for four hours.

Traveling in a motor home is a comfortable way to take a long road trip.

Many car travelers enjoy listening to music on the road. If everyone in the car can agree on the music, it can be nice to listen to it together. If not, headphones for the passengers will come in handy.

Today, some cars are equipped with screens to watch DVDs. Portable DVD players and other electronic devices also allow passengers to sit back and get comfortable with a movie or television show. But don't forget to look out the window every now and then, or else you might miss something interesting while watching the screen!

Documenting Your Trip
Sometimes the best records you have of a trip are your own descriptions of your experiences. Some travelers like to keep a journal to remember where they went and what they did. Online **blogs** are an easy way for a family to share a trip with friends and relatives at home.

Road Trip Necessities

One challenge for road travelers is to find the best possible places to sleep and eat. Roadside restaurants and hotels offer many services for travelers, but they can definitely vary in price and quality. A simple inn does not offer the same experience as a fancy hotel. Likewise, a fast-food restaurant will not appeal to people who prefer healthy, home-cooked meals.

So how can a person who is unfamiliar with an area find out about a particular **locality** (loh-KAL-i-tee)? There are many ways to do this kind of research. Some of it can even be done before you leave home. Using the Internet is a smart place to start your research. Many web sites are dedicated to rating restaurants and hotels.

Asking other people for their opinions can be the best type of research you could do. You can ask people that you know who have traveled to similar areas. You can even ask local people whom you meet on your trip. Firsthand recommendations can definitely steer you in the right direction.

Hotel Options
Hotels can offer certain **amenities** (uh-MEN-i-teez) to make a road trip easier. If they offer free Internet access, travelers can use it to do research on the stops they have planned on their trips. If the hotel offers free breakfast, that is one less meal that must be purchased on the road.

Road trips are much more **prevalent** (PREV-uh-luhnt) in places where automobile travel is common. In some countries around the world, people may not have access to cars. In those places, taking a train, bus, or plane is a more realistic way for people to travel on vacations.

A road trip requires roads and distance. Some regions are quite small or heavily populated. In these areas, people are not able to drive on an open highway for hundreds of miles. Other places do not even have paved roadways. For example, Venice, Italy, stretches across more than 100 islands and has waterways instead of roads in many places. Those types of locations would make it challenging to have a road trip adventure.

vintage train of Tierra del Fuego, Argentina

a double-decker bus in London, England

Grand Canal, Venice, Italy

You can use a proportion to convert one rate of speed to another. To find the equivalent of 40 miles per hour in feet per hour, multiply one rate by another.

Make sure the same unit of measure appears as the numerator of one fraction and the denominator of the other.

$$\frac{40 \text{ miles}}{1 \text{ hour}} \cdot \frac{5{,}280 \text{ feet}}{1 \text{ mile}} = 211{,}200 \text{ feet per hour}$$

When you divide 40 miles by 1 mile, the answer is 40. The unit of measure "cancels," leaving just a number. The answer, then, is in feet per hour, since those are the remaining units of measure.

LET'S EXPLORE MATH

a. A car is traveling at 60 mph. What is its speed in miles per day? (*Hint:* Think of how many hours are in a day.)

b. A truck is moving at 4,840 feet per minute. What is the speed in mph? (*Hint:* Think of how many minutes are in an hour and how many feet are in a mile.)

c. A car in Peru is traveling at 100 kilometers per hour. There are approximately 1.6 kilometers in a mile. About how fast is the car going in mph?

An important part of any road trip is having a **budget** so that you know how much money you can spend on trip expenses. One thing you can definitely expect to budget for on a road trip is the cost of gas. The distance of your trip, the type of car that you drive, and the price of gas all affect how much you will spend on gas for your trip.

Spending nights in hotels along the way will also be an expense to include in the budget. Some travelers choose to camp or stay with family or friends instead. This lowers the expenses in their budgets.

Food costs will depend on the types of restaurants that you choose. It can be cheaper (and healthier) to pack your own food and have a picnic. This is always a nice way to see parks and other outdoor spots of interest along the way.

Cruising Saves Money!
Using the cruise-control feature can make a car more fuel efficient. Cruise control is a system that automatically controls the speed of a car. It can help save money by keeping the speed steady.

LET'S EXPLORE MATH

The Mendoza family is on a road trip in New Zealand. Write a proportion to solve the following problems:

a. The family spent about $20 to put 10 liters of gasoline in their car. If they spent about $500 on gas for the road trip, about how many liters of gas did they purchase for the trip?

b. The Mendozas budgeted $250 for every two nights of lodging. If they need lodging for eight nights of their trip, how much did they budget for lodging?

c. The Mendozas' car uses 11 liters of gas per 100 kilometers. How many liters will be used to travel 250 kilometers?

Fuel Efficiency

Gas mileage is an example of a rate. It is the number of miles traveled per gallon (kilometers per liter) of gasoline burned. The gas mileage that your car gets will determine how often you will need to fill your tank. Some cars use gas much faster, while other models are more efficient at using fuel.

Off We Go!

Now you are ready to plan your own road trip! Think about where you want to go and consider how to make the trip more interesting. Make sure that you plan ahead and think things through before you leave. Many road trip travelers believe that it is the journey, rather than the destination, that should be enjoyed to the fullest.

Guangxi, China

Provence, France

Big Sur, California

Cape Town, South Africa

São Paolo, Brazil

    When you take a road trip, you can experience people and places in a whole new way. You can take your time and really enjoy the scenery and the appeal of a new location. You can chat with locals and find out about the best places to visit and sights to see. You can change your plans to make it the trip that you want. You are in charge of your vacation, so hit the road and have some fun!

Problem-Solving Activity

Midtown Auto Sales

Mrs. Lee, owner of Midtown Auto Sales, looked at the last two years of sales at her car dealership. She noticed an increase in hybrid car sales and would like to increase the amount of hybrids she has on the car lot. In order to do that, she must first decrease the amount of other types of cars that the dealership has in stock. Use the table below to answer the questions. Simplify your answers. Round percents to the nearest whole percent.

Midtown Auto Sales History 2011–2012

Car Type	2011 Sales	2012 Sales
sedan	320	285
sports car	103	72
truck	145	100
SUV	210	141
hybrid	90	156

Solve It!

a. What is the ratio of sales of hybrids to total cars in 2011? In 2012?

b. What percentage of sales was hybrids in 2011? In 2012?

c. What car type would you recommend Mrs. Lee decrease based on the 2011–2012 sales history?

d. Suppose Mrs. Lee's hybrid sales increased to 168 hybrids in 2013, and that total sales of cars increased in the same proportion from 2012 to 2013. How many cars would she have sold in 2013?

Use the steps below to help you answer the questions.

Step 1: Add the sales of all cars in 2011 and put that number under the number of hybrid cars. Simplify your answer by dividing both numbers by the same number. Repeat for 2012 sales.

Step 2: Write a sentence in the form _____ is _____% of _____. Use a proportion to solve the problem.

Step 3: Think about which car types had low percentages of sales from 2011–2012. Calculate the percentages to verify your answer.

Step 4: Write a proportion to solve the problem. Use the ratio of number of hybrids to number of total cars sold in 2012 on one side of the proportion. Use the ratio of number of hybrids sold to *x* on the other side of the proportion.

Glossary

amenities—things that make life easier or more pleasant

blogs—websites that are usually maintained by an individual who posts regular entries of commentary or other material

budget—a plan for how money will be spent during a particular period or for a particular purchase

commute—to travel regularly to and from a place, especially between home and work

desolate—isolated or deserted

discount—a percent or fraction of the original price that is subtracted to determine a sale price

economy—the wealth and resources of a particular area

equivalent ratios—two ratios that have the same value when simplified

expenses—money spent on goods or services

gas mileage—the rate of the distance traveled per amount of gasoline burned, generally expressed in miles per gallon (kilometers per liter)

global positioning system (GPS)—a navigation system that allows people to determine their exact location

locality—a particular place or area

percent—a part of a whole expressed in hundredths

prevalent—common or widespread

proportion—an equation showing two equivalent ratios

rate—a ratio comparing an amount or distance to a period of time

ratio—a comparison of two quantities

routes—paths or roads for traveling from one place to another

Index

amenities, 21

blog, 19

budget, 24–25

cartographer, 8

cross-multiplication, 12

cruise control, 24

discount, 15

economy, 17

equivalent ratios, 7

extremes in a proportion, 10, 12

gas mileage, 25

global positioning system (GPS), 9

means of a proportion, 10, 12

percent, 14–15, 28–29

proportion, 10–15, 18, 25, 29

rate, 13, 23, 25

ratio, 6–7, 11, 13–14, 18, 29

route, 5

speed, 13, 23–24

Answer Key

Let's Explore Math

Page 7:

a. 8:9; 3:2; 4:3

b. No; They are reciprocals.

c. 230 vehicles

d. 8:23; 23:9

e. It is important to express a ratio in words so that you know what each number in the ratio refers to.

Page 11:

a. 3:2; 2:3; 3:5; 2:5

b. 225 blue cars; Students should write a proportion like $\frac{3}{2} = \frac{b}{150}$.

c. 96 green cars; Students should write a proportion like $\frac{2}{5} = \frac{g}{240}$.

d. 144 blue cars; You could subtract 96 from 240 or solve the proportion $\frac{3}{5} = \frac{b}{240}$.

Page 13:

a. $\frac{168 \text{ miles}}{5 \text{ hours}}$, $\frac{33.6 \text{ miles}}{1 \text{ hour}}$

b. $\frac{168}{5} = \frac{n}{12}$; 403.2 miles

c. $\frac{168}{5} = \frac{190}{n}$; 6 hours

Page 15:

a. $18.75

b. 40%

Page 23:

a. 1,440 miles per day

b. 55 mph

c. 62.5 mph

Page 25:

a. Students should write a proportion like $\frac{20}{10} = \frac{500}{x}$; 250 liters

b. Students should write a proportion like $\frac{250}{2} = \frac{x}{8}$; $1,000

c. $\frac{11}{100} = \frac{x}{250}$; 27.5 liters

Problem-Solving Activity

a. 45:434; 78:377

b. 10%; 21%

c. Sports cars had the lowest average percentage of sales for the two years, so Mrs. Lee might want to decrease her sports car inventory.

d. A total of 812 cars would be sold in 2013.